May 2001

Vancouver
THE SECOND CENTURY

to Meg

some Pictures of our Hometown

with Love from
Ilse

NATURAL COLOR PRODUCTIONS
#17-1610 DERWENT WAY
DELTA BC V3M 6W1
Telephone: (604) 521-1579
www.naturalcolor.com

Vancouver
The Second Century

Vancouver, where dawn's promise is one of beauty and energy; where past, present and future are embodied in a single graceful entity. It is a city whose man-made structures enhance and reflect the striking loveliness that nature has bestowed upon its surroundings.

Hewn from a forest of massive firs, hemlocks and cedars, and spurred into growth by 19th century gold rushes and the coming of the railroad, Vancouver now enters its second century as a proud chieftain of commerce and as one of the world's most beautiful cities.

Since its mid-nineteenth century beginnings, the city has been a magnet, drawing people from all over the world. Today, poised at the gateway to the Pacific Rim, Vancouver has a distinctive cosmopolitan flavour.

The City

Vancouver is a place of sea and sky and wonderful reflections. The harbour views exhibit a blend of old and new architectural styles, mirroring the influences that continue to shape the city. English Bay serves as an antechamber to the Port of Vancouver, the largest port on the western coast of the Americas.

A modern cruise ship terminal at Canada Place welcomes visitors from around the world in stylish elegance. This multi-use facility also contains the World Trade Centre, Vancouver Trade and Convention Centre, Pan-Pacific Hotel, restaurants, shops and the exciting CN Imax Theatre.

To the left of Canada Place is the towering megalith of Granville Square, where the Port of Vancouver offices are located. Further left is the heritage Canadian Pacific Railway Station. The present building was built in 1912, on the site where the original wood-frame terminus was erected to welcome the first transcontinental train in 1887. Today it operates as the downtown SeaBus and SkyTrain terminus.

Above: The Vancouver skyline from Kitsilano Beach, looking across English Bay. Right: The polished bronze reflection of the water-front along Burrard Inlet, with Canada Place at the far right.

4

Since 1886, when farsighted citizens set aside the land, Stanley Park has delighted millions of people seeking refuge from the hustle of urban life. A wide range of facilities, landscapes and activities is available in the 405-hectare (over 1,000 acres) piece of paradise. Stanley Park is the largest urban park in Canada, and the second-largest in North America, surpassed in size only by New York City's Central Park.

The striking geodesic dome of the Expo Centre, a legacy of Expo '86, adds yet another fascinating facet to Vancouver's skyline. The Arts, Science and Technology Centre will have scientific exhibits for all ages and interests. Don't miss a chance to see the Omnimax Theatre, a unique way of viewing the world around us and the mysteries of the universe.

Right: Prospect Point in Stanley Park. The thickly forested North Shore mountains form an impressive backdrop to the city. The open arms of the Thunderbird figure on the totem and the fortuitous rainbow welcome visitors and residents alike to this enchanting spot. Below: Rowers take their exercise amid the glowing fall colours in Stanley Park. Opposite: Looking across False Creek, the geodesic panels on the Expo Centre reflect the last rays of the setting sun, while the rising moon casts its pale light over the city, highlighting the snowy peaks of the North Shore mountains.

The original settlement on the north shore of Burrard Inlet was Moodyville, founded in 1864 by Sewell Prescott Moody, when he took over the sawmill there. Unlike the "diamond in the rough" on the other side of Burrard Inlet, Moodyville was a more orderly company town. Affectionately known as "Sue," Moody provided services and facilities for the community's residents, resulting in the first school and electricity in the region.

As the area became increasingly industrialized with the growth of the timber and shipping industries, its isolation from the south shore of Burrard Inlet became acute. The Guinness brewing family, which had invested heavily in elite residential properties in West Vancouver, constructed the Lions Gate Bridge, opened by King George VI and Queen Elizabeth in 1939.

The timber companies and prairie grain producers soon saw to it that Vancouver's port facilities developed to handle the immense tonnage required of it. In 1987, over 60 million tonnes of cargo went through the harbour—to over 90 foreign countries. Vancouver's port ranks as one of the top 20 in the world.

Below: The picturesque village of Deep Cove in North Vancouver is nestled between Mt. Seymour and Indian Arm. The protected cove is home to many colourful species of waterfowl and the occasional noisy seal, splashing playfully in its calm waters. **Right:** *Burrard Inlet's First Narrows, spanned by the Lions Gate Bridge.*

8

Top left: *Stormy seas off West Vancouver are a great place for a yacht race, especially with Hollyburn and Grouse mountains as an impressive backdrop.* **Bottom left:** *The SeaBus leaving the terminal for Lonsdale Quay in North Vancouver, under the equally impressive backdrop of Vancouver's skyline.* **Right:** *Canada Place, its wonderfully illuminated sails stand out in the deep amethyst twilight.* **Following pages:** *Gold, copper and bronze reflections of Vancouver's skyline as seen from Stanley Park.*

Captain Vancouver sailed into local waters in 1792. He circumnavigated Vancouver Island and charted the mainland's intricate coastline. After mapping and surveying parts of what is now downtown Vancouver, he returned to England and thus set the stage for the explorers, traders and developers of the next century. The City of Vancouver was born in what is now called "Gastown," grew in a rapid and gangly fashion, and was incorporated in 1886. A raging fire razed the townsite that same year but, like the legendary phoenix, it rose from its ashes to become the glowing, energetic metropolis it is today. City Hall, located at 12th and Cambie streets, was built in 1936. The million-dollar structure was financed in a period of economic hard times by a special bond drive. City Hall's (then) modernistic design sports Art Deco elements on its facade, along with modernized neoclassical design features, such as the various friezes and columns.

Left: Vancouver has nearly 150 public parks and gardens. With its year-round mild climate and its stunning natural setting, it is one of the world's most desirable cities to live in or visit. **Above:** *Vancouver's dignified City Hall, with Captain George Vancouver's statue in front.*

Above: The Hotel Vancouver, old B.C. Courthouse—now the Vancouver Art Gallery—and Robson Square, in the heart of downtown Vancouver. **Above right:** Flags and fountain in Granville Square. The Art Deco architectural style of the Marine Building on the far right contrasts with contemporary office building styles. **Right:** B.C. Place Stadium, adds yet another shape to Vancouver's colourful and varied profile.

Vancouver's downtown offers an exciting array of architectural styles, both contemporary and historic. The prestigious Vancouver Art Gallery, adjacent to Robson Square, was once the B.C. Courthouse. Erected in 1909, it was designed by Sir Francis Rattenbury in the neoclassical style that was so popular at the turn of the century. The elegant Hotel Vancouver at Burrard and Georgia streets was started in 1926, but the Great Depression took its toll on many things, including urban development. A Canadian National Railway hotel, it was finally completed in 1939, the year of the Royal Visit by King George VI and Queen Elizabeth. Robson Square is a testament to liveable urban design. It boasts open, airy spaces that invite relaxed enjoyment of our downtown core. The Marine Building at 335 Burrard Street has long been one of Vancouver's favourite buildings. Built in 1929, and designed in the best Art Deco tradition, it was Vancouver's tallest building in its day. Don't miss the elaborate detail of the lobby. As a contrasting, but no less dramatic architectural achievement, the B.C. Place Stadium adds yet another dimension to the city. Built in 1983, it covers 10 acres of prime downtown property, holds 60,000 spectators and is the home of the B.C. Lions football team.

Canada Place was opened in May 1986, after nearly three years of construction, as the Canada Pavilion for Expo '86. The five graceful sails are made from a teflon-coated fibreglass fabric and are suspended by 10 steel masts that rise 80 feet. At the time of its completion in 1985, it was the largest fabric tension structure in the world. A rainbow of coloured lights plays across the translucent sails on special occasions. The Pan-Pacific Hotel offers truly opulent accommodation to guests from around the world. Over $3\frac{1}{2}$ acres of bird's-eye maple was used in finishing its interior. The Indian rose marble throughout was polished in Italy. The entire complex is an artistic achievement and a joy to explore. One of Vancouver's most interesting backdrops is Mt. Baker, in the Washington Cascades, sometimes seen clearly, as in the picture above, and sometimes seen as an ethereal presence, hovering in mid-air over banks of wispy clouds. Occasionally, in the clear early light of dawn, a feather of steam from one of its dormant volcanic vents may be visible.

Left: Cruise ships, yachts, even a paddlewheeler, at rest at the elegant Canada Place terminus. *Above:* Pan-Pacific Hotel in the Canada Place complex. The majestic snow-capped volcanic cone of Mt. Baker appears in the background beside the hotel.

Looking like a giant flying saucer, the Planetarium produces popular programs—entertaining and educational. The projector can show the sky from any latitude on earth at any time: past, present or future. The Vancouver Museum's galleries present regional history in artful displays. The crab sculpture at the entrance has a time capsule beneath it that will be opened in the year 2067. Native legend says that the crab is the guardian of the harbour. The nearby Maritime Museum displays the marine history of the region. Also located here is the St. Roch National Historic Site. This 140-foot vessel was the first to navigate the northwest passage in both directions. Heritage Harbour has a collection of antique sailing vessels, showing the fine craftsmanship of the early days.

Left: The H.R. MacMillan Planetarium and Vancouver Museum, in Vanier Park. **Top:** Heritage Harbour at the Maritime Museum on Ogden Street. **Bottom:** Mural on the west wall of the Maritime Museum depicts a collage of maritime artifacts and lore.

The Museum of Anthropology at UBC opened its magnificent doors to the public in 1976. Artifacts are displayed in gallery settings, as the works of fine art they are. The collection of Northwest Coast Indian art is truly astounding. The list of items includes house boards and poles, totem poles, feast dishes, kerfed storage boxes, argillite carvings, gold and silver jewellry, masks, rattles and weaving tools. The cultures represented include Coast Salish, Bella Bella, Haida, Tsimshian, Tlingit, Kwakiutl and Nootka. One amazing exhibit is a larger-than-life-size yellow cedar carving depicting the Haida legend of Raven and the First People. The Museum of Anthropology is world-famous for its public programmes and display techniques. This is a treat not to be missed on any visit to Vancouver.

Right: Totem Pole and longhouse at the UBC Museum of Anthropology. Bottom: Gallery of totems fittingly housed in Arthur Erickson's award-winning architectural design. Far right: Clock tower on the University of British Columbia campus. UBC is British Columbia's largest and oldest provincial university. Following pages: Aerial view showing off Vancouver, like a jewel in its scintillating setting.

Granville Island

When the Canadian Pacific Railway built its terminal here in 1885, the False Creek region rapidly became the industrial heart of the city. The demand for land was so great that a third of this inlet was filled in, creating Granville Island in 1915. Redeveloped in the 1970s, the results are here for all to enjoy: residences, galleries, restaurants, theatres and an exciting public market. Fresh produce, fish and seafood, meats, plants and other groceries are available Tuesday through Sunday.

Left: *Granville Island and the Granville Street Bridge, with Vancouver and the snow-dusted North Shore mountains in the background.* **Above:** *Granville Island Public Market.*

27

Gastown

Logging, mills, shipping—the cornerstones of Vancouver's permanent settlement—were industries that employed thousands of men. When Jack Deighton arrived in 1867, he brought with him a commodity he knew he could market: a barrel of whiskey. This enterprising British steamboat pilot and prospector opened up a bar and restaurant—an excellent forum for his habit of regaling his customers with many a tall tale. Nicknamed "Gassy" Jack, the area around his Globe Saloon soon came to be called Gastown. It flourished in a rather boisterous fashion, and was renamed Granville—the heart of old Vancouver. When Canadian Pacific Rail developed its terminal away from Gastown, it fell into a decline. Faithful renovation of this historic area during the recent period of urban renewal has enabled Gastown to regain some of its former glory. It now boasts several restaurants, shops and nightspots to entertain both visitors and residents.

Far left: The Gastown Steam Clock at the corner of Cambie and Water streets. Above left: "Gassy" Jack Deighton, after whom Gastown is named. Below: Water Street— Gastown's main thoroughfare.

Chinatown

The area now called Chinatown was the home of some of Vancouver's earliest pioneers. It is one of the oldest commercial and residential districts in the city.

Below: *Dragon Parade in one of Chinatown's exciting celebrations.* **Right:** *Neon brilliance of a restaurant's marquee.* **Bottom:** *Pender Street in Chinatown, a place of exotic restaurants, shops and markets.* **Opposite page:** *Dr. Sun Yat-Sen Classical Chinese Gardens. An enchanting universe of solitude hidden away in the bustling downtown core.*

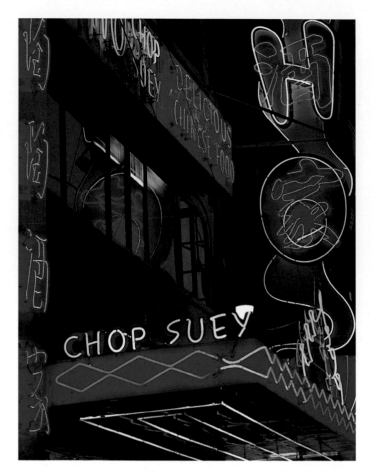

Gardens of the City

The mild climate of southwestern B.C. encourages the growth of a fantastic number of plant species. Gardeners go wild in this region, and nowhere is it more apparent than in Queen Elizabeth Park. Named for the Queen Mother, this nearly 140-acre park is located atop Little Mountain, in the geographical centre of Vancouver. From its height, there is a 360-degree panoramic view of the city. Underneath the 43-metre dome over 400 species of plants flourish in desert and lush tropical climates. The addition of 50 different kinds of birds increases the enjoyment of a visit here. Initially the quarry site for materials for Vancouver's first roads, the once ugly scar has been transformed by city horticultural crews into marvellous ornamental gardens. There are also 20 tennis courts.

Above: *Inside the dome at the Bloedel Conservatory.*
Right: *Gardens and the conservatory's triodetic dome at Queen Elizabeth Park.*

Among Vancouver's nearly 150 parks, Queen Elizabeth Park ranks second only to Stanley Park as a favourite. The plants were collected from around the world thanks to the Bloedel family, which also financed the triodetic dome. Two reservoirs for the city's drinking water are in the park, one beneath the dome and the other under the tennis courts. Queen Elizabeth Park and Bloedel Conservatory are located at 33rd and Cambie streets.

Once a fashionable Shaughnessy golf course, the Van Dusen Botanical Gardens at 37th and Oak are 55 acres of horticultural wizardry. Exquisitely designed and displayed, a variety of ecological zones are exhibited, each with their major plant species. Rhododendrons are a popular feature, as are the many interesting large stone sculptures throughout. Educational and other programs for all ages are featured throughout the year.

Right: Exquisite spring flower beds in Queen Elizabeth Park. Below: From atop Little Mountain the outstanding natural setting of Vancouver can be appreciated. The Grouse Mountain ski area and twin peaks of the Lions can be seen over in the North Shore. Opposite page: Basking in the warm, burnished copper glow of sunset, the Bloedel Conservatory provides a warm climate in any weather.

The Van Dusen Gardens is the site of MacMillan Bloedel's "A Walk in the Forest" exhibit. Tours are provided to give visitors a better understanding of trees and forest ecology.

Top: A tranquil setting in Van Dusen Gardens shows off an ingenious combination of native and introduced plants. Bottom: How inviting—to sit in the shade of a friendly tree. Opposite page: Fantasy Gardens in Richmond is a delightful refuge of flowers, garden statuary, windmills and family fun.

Officially opened in June, 1960, this special garden is a memorial to a great man of peace, Dr. Inazo Nitobe. Designed by Dr. Kannosuke Mori of Japan, a distinguished Japanese professor of landscape architecture, this 1-hectare site is a remarkable tribute to peace and Japanese-Canadian relations. While many of the plants and materials have come from Japan, Dr. Mori realized that our forests were similar and that we shared an appreciation of the broad-leaved evergreen shrubs, azaleas and flowering cherries. Our native pines could be trained in the traditional Japanese fashion, so there was no need to import them. The fine-leaved Japanese maples, however, were purchased in Japan, and add a wonderful sense of colour throughout the year, their leaves changing from a delicate green in spring to vibrant vermilion in autumn. Two major types of Japanese gardens are illustrated here: a large, informal garden to stroll through, and a small, intimate tea garden—for quiet reflection— within it.

Left: The quintessential Japanese garden, Nitobe Memorial Garden, is located on the UBC campus adjacent to the Asian Centre. Below: Cherry blossom time is particularly lovely in the Nitobe Memorial Garden.

39

Stanley Park

Vancouver Aquarium Marine Science Centre

Gleeful squeals, joy, wonderment, excitement and disbelief in the face of proof are all part of the experience of a visit to the Vancouver Aquarium in Stanley Park. One of the largest and most popular aquariums in North America, there is an encompassing range of high quality entertainment and educational programs, including important aquatic research, performed at the aquarium. Its live collection now contains some 6,000 specimens of mammals, reptiles, birds, amphibians, invertebrates and fishes. There are whale pools, seal and otter enclaves, a shark tank, freshwater fish galleries, an amazing coelocanth display, and the outstanding Amazon tropical gallery, as well as many other aspects of aquatic life. The Clam Shell gift shop has many interesting and attractive items, including books and artwork.

Previous pages: Killer whales performing at the Vancouver Aquarium. ***Opposite page:*** *The wonder of meeting face-to-face with such a magnificent creature is evident in this child's posture.* ***Top:*** *A white Beluga whale at the Aquarium.* ***Below:*** *Don't sit in the "Splash Zone" while these orcas are performing.*

The Zoo

The Zoo at Stanley Park is open every day and is free. Walking through this area of the park is an enjoyable experience, watching the faces of surprised visitors when an impertinent squirrel chitters demandingly for a peanut. Some of the Canada geese are as tall as the children here, and they, too, accompany us on our walks, honking and talking among themselves.

Opposite page: Sleek, mischievious river otters, for whom this fence serves no other purpose than as a prop. You may think you've come here to observe the animals, but who's observing whom here? **Left:** *Two small Adelie penguins contemplating a brisk dip in the pool.* **Bottom:** *Undisputed king of the arctic, the polar bear is powerful yet strangely non-threatening. An excellent example of the wonders of evolution, the polar bear is perfectly designed for his more aquatic, arctic habitat, exhibiting adaptive colouration, slightly webbed paws to swim more efficiently, and a streamlined body shape.*

Stanley Park is an all-season playground. Sports enthusiasts, fitness buffs, Sunday strollers and happy visitors are drawn to its scenic beauty and many excellent facilities.

*Opposite page: A group of totems in Stanley Park, sporting Thunderbird figures. **Top left:** A jogger runs along a portion of the seawall under the Lions Gate Bridge. **Below:** On another part of the seawall around Stanley Park, a fitness group takes their exercise. **Bottom:** A winter's walk in Stanley Park, as exquisitely etched as a Currier & Ives picture.*

Top: The city of Vancouver gleams like the proverbial pot of gold—beneath a double rainbow!
Lower: A gloriously sunny day on Jericho Beach in Kitsilano. Sunbathers and windsurfers flock to the beautiful beaches along English Bay on days like this.

Above: *Geometric shapes, starkly white against the water's deep blue reflection of the sky, are contrasted with the graceful life form of the gull, floating by ever so slowly on the thinnest breath of air.*

The North Shore

The North Shore stretches from Horseshoe Bay in the west, eastward to Deep Cove on Indian Arm. North and West Vancouver are its two primary municipalities. Behind them, and supplying the city of Vancouver with much of its fantastic backdrop, are the North Shore Mountains. Cypress Provincial Park, Grouse Mountain, Lynn Canyon Park and Mt. Seymour Provincial Park are here for year-round recreational enjoyment, offering all types of skiing, hiking, hang-gliding and nature appreciation experiences.

Above: *The Lions Gate Bridge at rush hour. The thickly forested North Shore slopes occupy the entire background.* **Right:** *The SeaBus gives a perfect vantage point to view the harbour and the spectacular North Shore skyline.* **Following pages:** *A stunning sunset silhouettes the mountains to the north. The Lions Gate Bridge glitters like a necklace of crystal beads strung across Burrard Inlet.*

At the top of Grouse Mountain is a marvellous panorama of Vancouver, the Gulf Islands and Vancouver Island, and sometimes a magical view of Mt. Baker, floating on the southeastern horizon. The facilities on Grouse are all world-class, from the lifts to the restaurants to the slopes.

Opposite page: The thrilling skyride up Grouse Mountain passes over a colourful array of subalpine wildflowers. **Left:** Skiing through the sunset on Grouse Mountain. **Below:** The Lions in winter, one of Vancouver's most popular—and famous —landmarks. **Bottom:** Skiing in the amethyst and gold richness of a winter's eve has got to be one of life's more rewarding experiences.

Capilano Suspension Bridge

This delightful place opened in 1899. There is a 15-acre park with trout and salmon ponds, and guided trails through the lush rainforest. Massive hemlock, spruce, fir and cedar trees blanket the steep slopes. An ancient Douglas fir measures at least 3.5 metres in girth, and all around are evergreen shrubs: huckleberries, oregon grape and salal. The sun-dappled atmosphere is a perfect complement to the thrilling, breath-catching experience of crossing the bridge. Millions of people have walked over this famous bridge. Gauzy, veil-like waterfalls cascade down the banks over polished rock chutes, creating moisture for small delicate ferns. The trading post is over 50 years old and is one of the largest craft stores in Canada. Full tour facilities include an outdoor barbecue and full-service restaurant. The suspension bridge is located on Capilano Road, close to the Capilano Salmon Hatchery and Grouse Mountain.

Left: The Capilano Suspension Bridge spans the gorge of the Capilano River, 230 feet above its often turbulent waters. *Inset photo:* Totem park and gardens at the entrance. *Below:* Swing and sway for 450 feet across the longest and oldest foot suspension bridge in the world.

Among three notable structures that can be seen are the geodesic dome of the Expo Centre, Canada Place and its luminescent sails, and B.C. Place Stadium. A great way to see the city from this height is to take the Superskyride at Grouse Mountain. This is Canada's largest and longest-operating mountain tramway. The Grouse Nest Restaurant on top offers elegant dining and evening entertainment.

Above: Aerial view of the city in the deep indigo of twilight.

Vancouver is one of the major centres from which to take a cruise—whether down to the sun -washed beaches of Mexico and Hawaii, or up to the midnight sun brilliance of Alaska—take your pick. The cruise north through the Inside Passage, however, is especially exciting, and offers the opportunity to view killer whales and other marine mammals, and to see magnificent glaciers, some calving directly into the ocean, leaving irridescent blue ice on the glacier's new face.

Top: A cruise ship sails into port past the highrises of West Vancouver. *Bottom:* Coming in with the tide and the rising sun, a cruise ship arrives in Vancouver's busy, exciting port.

On the Move

B.C. Transit's SeaBus plies the waters of busy Burrard Inlet on a regular basis. Fully integrated with the transit system, it carries people to the heart of downtown Vancouver. Put into service in June 1977, it is an efficient alternative to a third bridge across the inlet. The fleet's two vessels, the *Burrard Beaver* and the *Burrard Otter*, were built by Yarrows Shipbuilding of Victoria. These double-ended catamarans have a high level of stability and their independent drives allow them to be moved forwards, backwards, sideways and crabwise. They can be stopped within their own length, and with a speed of 13.5 knots, are effective rapid transport across Burrard Inlet.

Opposite page: The SeaBus crosses Burrard Inlet at frequent intervals. **Left:** *Taking advantage of strong winds, a brave windsurfer gets an excellent view of West Vancouver and its mountain backdrop.* **Bottom:** *The Royal Hudson Steam Train operates a tour up Howe Sound from North Vancouver to Squamish, from May to September. The authentically refurbished train includes an antique gleaming locomotive, open observation car, bar car and several passenger cars.*

This is a particularly lovely spot for a short trip, and you may see a whale or two on your crossing. The village of Gibson's Landing is a short distance up the Sunshine Coast. This is the town where the popular TV series "The Beachcombers" is filmed.

Guiding ships into Vancouver's harbour for decades, the Point Atkinson Lighthouse sits atop the weathered, glacier-scoured bedrock of this rocky shore.

Above: *Horseshoe Bay marina and B.C. Ferry landing for trips to Vancouver Island and up the Sunshine Coast.* **Right:** *B.C. Ferries coming and going at Horseshoe Bay.* **Following page:** *Point Atkinson Lighthouse at the bottom of Lighthouse Park in West Vancouver.*